LIFE IN AN
EGYPTIAN
TOWN

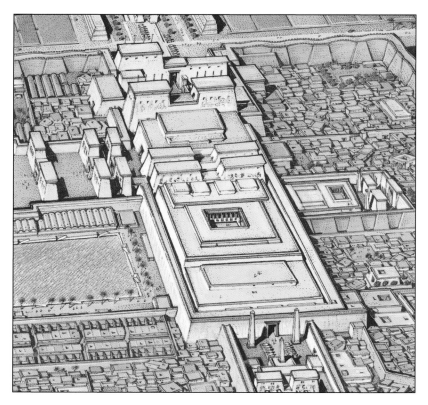

JANE SHUTER

Heinemann
LIBRARY

Produced for Heinemann Library by
   Bender Richardson White.
Photo research by Cathy Stastny and
   Maria Joannou
Designed by Ben White and
   Ron Kamen
Printed in China

09 08 07 06
10 9 8 7 6 5 4 3 2

**Library of Congress Cataloging-in-Publication
Data**

Shuter, Jane.
   Life in an Egyptian town / Jane Shuter.
      p. cm. — (Picture the past)
   Includes bibliographical references and index.
   ISBN 1-4034-5831-6 (hardcover) — ISBN 1-4034-
5839-1 (pbk.)
   1. Egypt—Social life and customs—To 332 B.C.—
Juvenile literature. 2. Cities and towns, Ancient—
Egypt—Juvenile literature. I. Title. II. Series.
   DT61.S6447 2004
   932—dc22

                                          2004002362

Acknowledgments
The publishers would like to thank the following
for permission to reproduce photographs:
Ancient Art and Architecture/John P. Stevens p.
25; Ancient Art and Architecture/R. Sheridan pp.
8, 12, 15; Committee of Egypt Exploration,
London p. **24**; Corbis Images Inc. p. **30**;
Heinemann Library pp. **16, 28**; Peter Evans p. **27**;
Robert Harding Picture Library p. **6**; Trustees of the
British Museum p. **18, 21, 22** (numbers EA10057/8-
PS177397, EA-15671-PS213448, EA26780-PS343512);
Werner Forman Archive/Dr. E. Strouhal p. **14, 17**;
Werner Forman Archive/Museo Egizio, Turin p.
23;Werner Forman Archive/The British Museum,
London p. **13** (number PH1033A); Werner Forman
Archive/The Egyptian Museum, Cairo pp. **7, 10,
19, 20, 26**.

Cover photograph of a wooden model of a
carpentry workshop with craftsmen at work
reproduced with permission of Werner Forman
Archive.

Every effort has been made to contact copyright
holders of any material reproduced in this book.
Any omissions will be rectified in subsequent
printings if notice is given to the publisher.

Some words are shown in bold, **like this**.
You can find out what they mean by
looking in the glossary.

ABOUT THIS BOOK

This book is about daily life in towns
in ancient Egyptian times, which
lasted from about 3100 B.C.E to 30
B.C.E. The ancient Egyptians lived in
towns and villages along the River
Nile. Most of Egypt is desert. The
climate is hot, with very little rain.
Ancient Egyptians could live in
Egypt only because the Nile gave
water for farming, drinking and
washing, and it flooded each year.
When the flooding went down, it left
behind rich soil for growing crops.
Towns and villages were always close
to the Nile, which was used for
transport, too. Many townspeople
were farmers.

We have illustrated this book with
photographs of objects from ancient
Egyptian times and artists' ideas of
town life. These drawings are based
on information about ancient
Egyptian towns that has been found
by **archaeologists**.

The author
Jane Shuter is a professional writer and
editor of non-fiction books for children.
She graduated from Lancaster University in
1976 with a BA honours degree and then
earned a teaching qualification. She taught
from 1976 to 1983, changing to editing and
writing when her son was born. She lives in
Oxford with her husband and son.

Contents

Egyptian Towns

Ancient Egyptian towns were large settlements. They were built in places where there were important **temples.** They also were built around palaces for the **pharaoh**, the ruler of Egypt, or where the **officials** who helped him to run the country lived. Towns were busy, noisy places. Tall houses were crowded together. The streets were dirty and smelly, too. They were full of garbage that people threw away, because there was no garbage collection.

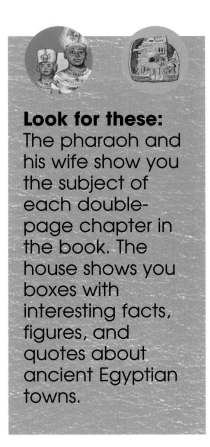

Look for these:
The pharaoh and his wife show you the subject of each double-page chapter in the book. The house shows you boxes with interesting facts, figures, and quotes about ancient Egyptian towns.

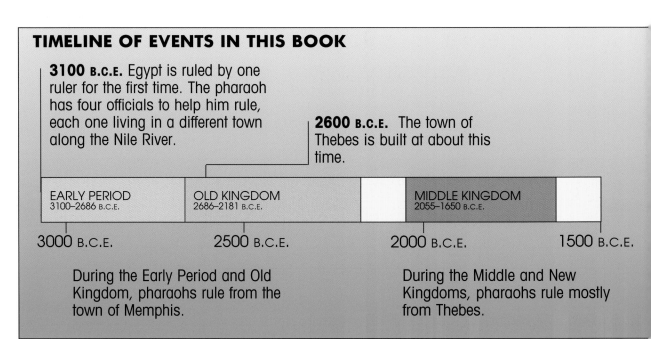

TIMELINE OF EVENTS IN THIS BOOK

3100 B.C.E. Egypt is ruled by one ruler for the first time. The pharaoh has four officials to help him rule, each one living in a different town along the Nile River.

2600 B.C.E. The town of Thebes is built at about this time.

| EARLY PERIOD 3100–2686 B.C.E. | OLD KINGDOM 2686–2181 B.C.E. | | MIDDLE KINGDOM 2055–1650 B.C.E. | |

3000 B.C.E. 2500 B.C.E. 2000 B.C.E. 1500 B.C.E.

During the Early Period and Old Kingdom, pharaohs rule from the town of Memphis.

During the Middle and New Kingdoms, pharaohs rule mostly from Thebes.

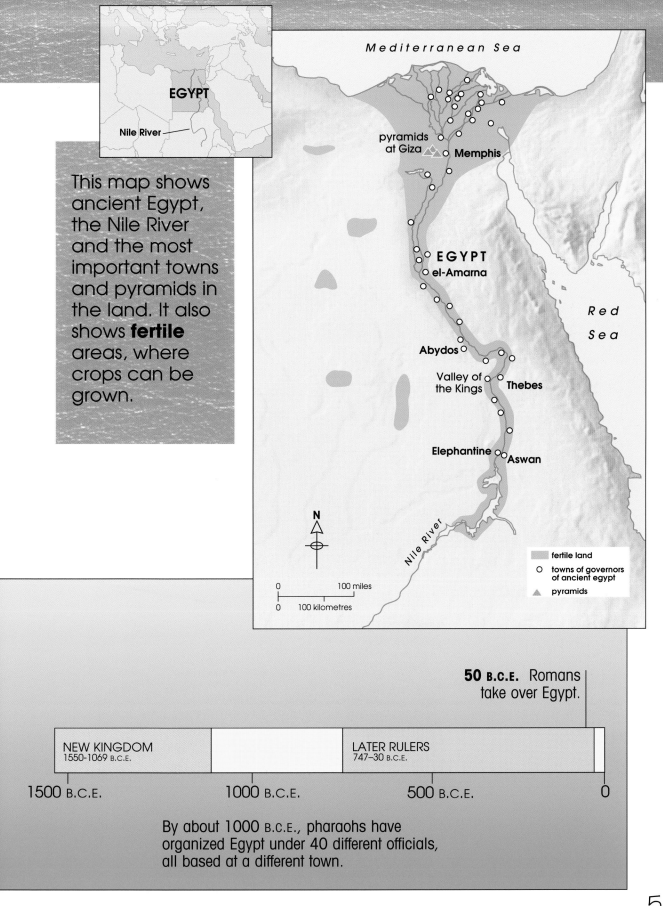

EGYPT

Nile River

Mediterranean Sea

pyramids
at Giza △△△ **Memphis**

EGYPT
el-Amarna

Red

Sea

Abydos ○

Valley of ○
the Kings **Thebes**

Elephantine ○○**Aswan**

Nile River

N

	fertile land
○	towns of governors of ancient egypt
△	pyramids

0   100 miles

0   100 kilometres

This map shows ancient Egypt, the Nile River and the most important towns and pyramids in the land. It also shows **fertile** areas, where crops can be grown.

50 B.C.E. Romans take over Egypt.

| NEW KINGDOM 1550-1069 B.C.E. | | LATER RULERS 747–30 B.C.E. | |

1500 B.C.E.   1000 B.C.E.   500 B.C.E.   0

By about 1000 B.C.E., pharaohs have organized Egypt under 40 different officials, all based at a different town.

The Pharaoh's Palaces

The **pharaoh** lived in a palace in the town he wanted to rule from—his main site, or capital. Thebes and Memphis were most often used as capitals.

Other big towns had palaces for the pharaoh to use as he traveled. Some **temples** also had palaces, built on one side of the temple buildings. This was because the pharaoh was the religious leader of Egypt, too. Palaces always had a wall around them, to keep them separate from the rest of the town.

Pharaohs owned valuable things that were buried with them when they died. This mask of gold and gemstones was put on the pharaoh Tutankhamun when he was buried in 1327 B.C.E.

The palace had many different rooms, gardens, and pools. Some parts of the palace were used only for important occasions, such as visits from foreign rulers. All the palace was beautifully decorated, inside and outside. The mud bricks were plastered over and painted white. Then they were painted with colorful scenes of birds in the marshes, or scenes that showed how powerful the pharaoh was.

MUD BRICKS

All ancient Egyptian houses were built from mud bricks— even the pharaoh's palaces. The only stone buildings were the temples, although stone was also used for the outside of some of the **pyramids** —the tombs of some of the pharaohs.

Ancient Egyptians, even pharaohs, did not have much furniture. But the furniture they did have was well made. This bed and chair belonged to the mother of the pharaoh Khufu.

Temples

Most towns had at least one **temple.** Temples were the only stone buildings. They were beautifully carved and painted. They were built as homes for the gods and goddesses of ancient Egypt. Some temples were huge, with their own workshops, workers' houses, and farmland. Others were no bigger than a house. Sometimes several gods and goddesses shared a temple. Most people could not go into temples. **Priests** and **priestesses** could go in, to serve the gods and goddesses.

TEMPLES

An ancient Egyptian carving on a temple describes how it was decorated, "The temple was built from white stone. The floors were lined with silver. Its doorways were decorated with a mixture of gold and silver."

In this painting, a sem-priest, on the left, is at a funeral. Sem-priests performed all the ceremonies at burials. They always wore a leopard skin—no other priest did.

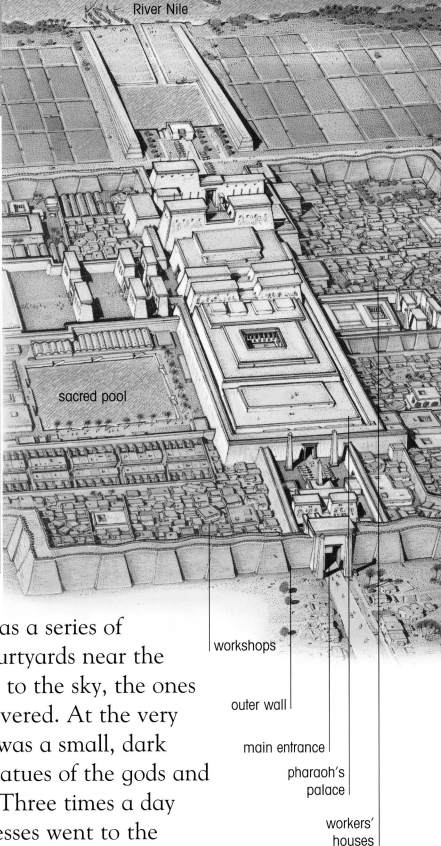

River Nile

This huge temple to many gods has:
- a wall around it
- courtyards in a line from the main entrance to the Nile River (in the back)
- a palace for the pharaoh, with its own outer wall
- a sacred pool, for the priests to wash in before worshipping the gods
- workshops and workers' houses.

sacred pool

workshops

outer wall

main entrance

pharaoh's palace

workers' houses

Temples were built as a series of **courtyards.** The courtyards near the entrance were open to the sky, the ones at the back were covered. At the very back of the temple was a small, dark **shrine** room with statues of the gods and goddesses inside it. Three times a day the priests or priestesses went to the temple to worship in front of the statues.

Shopping

Towns did not have shops. The ancient Egyptians lived simply and did not have many things. But they needed cooking pots, clothes, and baskets. People did not use money, but swapped spare food or things they had made for items they needed.

This trading is called bartering, and it was how all trade was carried out in ancient Egypt. People knew what things were worth related to the price of a lump of metal, usually copper or silver. Wealthy people had more food, land, animals, and belongings to trade.

Traders brought in expensive things from other countries, such as wood, jewels, spices, and animal skins. They brought them to the town by boats along the Nile. Only the pharaoh or wealthy people could afford expensive goods.

TRADE

When Hay, a worker at the town of Deir el-Medina, bought an ox from the local policeman, he traded it for:
- two jars of fresh fat
- five tunics of smooth cloth
- a skirt of thin cloth
- an animal skin.

Sometimes people bartered with neighbors and friends. If a friend did not have a spare **tunic,** ox, or basket to trade, they may have known someone who did. But people also bartered at markets that were held often, usually at the docks by the river, where there was a big open space. People put out what they had to barter on mats on the ground.

Markets like this one were held in the open air. People often put up cloth **awnings** to give them some shade from the sunlight.

Homes

Ancient Egyptian homes were built to deal with the hot, dry weather. They were made of mud bricks. Town houses were built two or three stories high, and close together in rows.

Houses had small, high windows with wooden shutters and openings in the roof to let in some air. Inside, rooms were often dark and cramped, and had very little furniture. Everyone used their roof as a living space. People spent more time on the roof, often under an **awning,** than indoors.

Wealthy people had gardens with ponds, like the one shown on this ancient Egyptian wall painting . Like gardens, ponds were expected to be useful as well as nice to look at. People ate the fish and ducks that lived in them.

Because there was less space in towns, people who wanted a lot of room had to build upward, so there were many tall, thin houses. This is a model of a house with three stories, found in a tomb.

Most people painted their homes white inside. Wealthier people had more rooms, more furniture, and more space. They had fancy wall paintings, especially in the room they used for entertaining. They had toilets and washrooms, but no drains. They collected the washing water and toilet waste to put on the fields. Most people just used the fields as toilets and washed in the river.

Using the River

The ancient Egyptians built most of their towns close to the Nile River because they needed its water every day. The flooding of the Nile gave them the rich, muddy soil to grow their crops, which needed daily watering from the river, too. The ancient Egyptians used water from the Nile to make the bread and beer everyone ate and drank. Workers needed water to make mud bricks and clay pots. People washed, bathed, and swam in the river.

LAUNDRY

Most people had someone else wash for them, as homes did not have running water. Washing was done in the river, by men only. A **scribe** wrote, "The washerman washes on the shore, while the crocodile lurks nearby." Laundry was a dangerous job.

Bakers made dough from grain flour and water from the Nile. They kneaded the dough, then placed it in clay molds. Then they baked them in ovens heated by burning wood.

The Nile River provided food as well as water. The ancient Egyptians ate fish and wild birds more often than they ate farm animals, such as sheep and cattle. The Nile was also the most important way of traveling around Egypt, as towns were built along the river. Even short journeys were by boat because there were few roads or tracks through the desert.

Boats were an important way for people to go up and down the Nile River. People also needed them to cross the river, as there were no bridges. Boatmen ran regular ferry trips across.

Work

Every big town had craft workshops for potters, furniture makers, metalworkers, glassmakers, weavers, leather workers, and jewelers. Men did these jobs. Women from wealthy families took care of their homes and children. Women from poorer families worked as servants, or in spinning and weaving workshops. They also worked baking bread and brewing beer.

The most skillful workers worked in the big workshops that belonged to the **pharaoh** or to important **officials,** or worked in **temples.**

Most townspeople, whatever their jobs, worked for the temple or the important town officials, or even the pharaoh. As well as their ordinary work, everyone who was not a **scribe** had to do **duty work** for the pharaoh. This was often building work, hauling stone for temples or tombs, or constructing new houses in the town.

Making bricks was an important job in ancient Egypt. Houses and palaces were built from mud bricks, which crumbled over time in the heat. They often needed repairing. Brickmakers mixed mud and straw together, then pressed the mixture down into a wooden frame. Most bricks were dried out in the hot sunlight.

All towns needed brickmakers. Their mud bricks were similar in size to the gray concrete blocks that house builders use today on the insides of walls.

Education

This is part of the ancient Egyptian *Rhind Mathematical Papyrus,* which was used to teach scribes. It shows how to figure out the angles of **pyramids.**

In ancient Egypt, most children did not go to school. Reading and writing were skills that only the children of **scribes** were taught. These boys and girls were taught from the age of five, at a school in the **temple** or in a town **official**'s home. They were learning to run the country for the **pharaoh,** so they had to learn math, too.

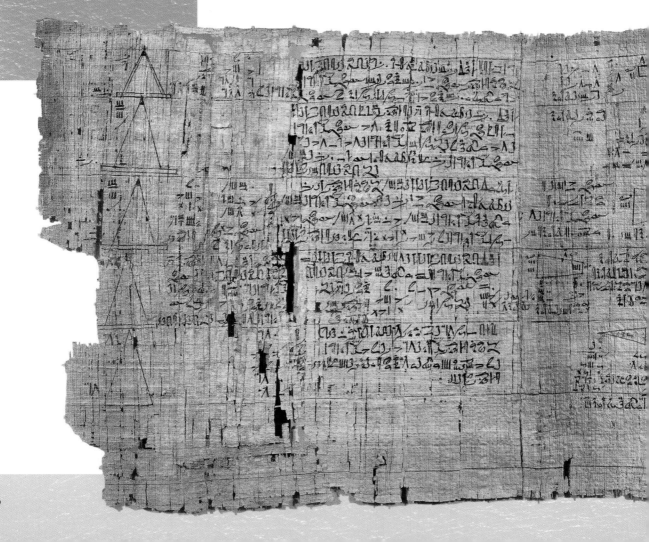

MATH

Usually, boys learned their father's job. From the age of about five, the sons of craftsmen began to help their fathers at work in the home. They fetched and carried, then did simple tasks. A few years later, most of them would become **apprentices** in the workshops where their fathers worked.

Mothers taught girls how to run a home. If their mothers worked in a bakery or a weaving workshop, girls sometimes learned this skill, too.

This ancient Egyptian model shows a weaving workshop where all the workers were women. Weaving was one of the few **trades** that women were allowed to do.

Play

Even though children started to work from the age of five, they still played together in their spare time. Ordinary children in towns spent a lot of time playing together outside, not in their cramped homes. They played with balls made from pieces of leather stitched together and stuffed with dried grass. Some of these balls have survived from 2,500 years ago. Most pictures from the time show boys playing separately from girls.

Some tomb models show children at work, like the two boys (top right) in this furniture-makers' workshop. The boys would have begun work by sweeping up the workshop and fetching and carrying for the older workers.

GAMES

The **pharaoh's** children did not play on the streets with other children. They played in the palace. Children from important families played at home, too. Their homes had more space and yards to play in. The girls had beautiful dolls made from wood, with arms and legs that moved. Girls from ordinary families had stiff wooden dolls, or dolls made from clay.

Many outdoor games in ancient Egypt were similar to those played today. Children raced each other and played chasing games. An ancient Egyptian carving showing boys playing tug-of-war has one boy shouting to the other, "My side is stronger than yours!"

This toy once belonged to the child of an important family. The string makes the cat's mouth open and close.

Clothes

Egypt is very hot, so all Egyptians dressed to keep cool. Children wore nothing but sandals until about the age of ten. Everyone else wore clothes made from **linen.** Townspeople and villagers wore the same kinds of clothes. Working men just wore a short piece of cloth wrapped around their hips like a short skirt, or tucked between their legs like baggy underpants. Ordinary women wore a **tunic** to at least their knees.

JEWELRY

Men, women and children wore jewelry. Poor people wore copper rings or a string of beads. The wealthier a person was, the more jewelry they wore. They wore jeweled belts, earrings, rings, bracelets, and collars —wide, flat necklaces that closed at the back.

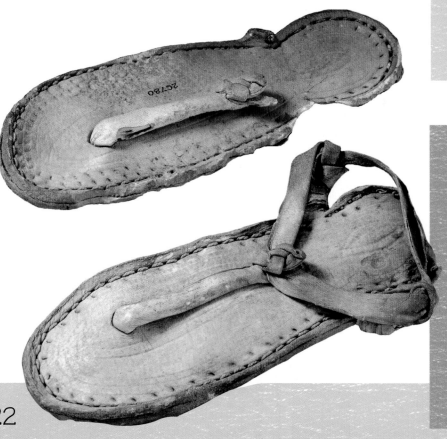

Only the leather sandals worn by wealthy people have survived for us to study. Most people wore sandals made from old reeds or other plant stems —or they went barefoot.

People kept their makeup in pots stored in wooden boxes, or in baskets.
This painted box belonged to a wealthy lady.

Wealthy people wore thinner linen cloth, bleached white to reflect the sun and keep the wearer cooler. The thin cloth took longer to make. Women wore long tunics, and men wore tunics that came to the knees or to the ground. Often these clothes had lots of folds and pleats. They were harder to move freely in, and were more likely to get caught on things. They were for people who did not have to do hard work.

Wealthy people wore lots of makeup and jewelry. Ordinary townspeople and villagers could not afford makeup and had only cheap jewelry.

Health and Hygiene

The ancient Egyptians believed in keeping clean. They washed daily with water from the river, and washed their clothes often. They often shaved their heads, sometimes their whole bodies, with razors made from **bronze.** Many homes had a bathroom where people stood on a stone slab and poured water over themselves. They had no soap, but scrubbed themselves with a salt called natron. The water drained into a big bowl and was emptied on the fields.

Only wealthy people had a stone toilet seat like this one. Most were made of wood. The seat was laid over a pottery jar that was emptied at least once a day. Poor people had no toilets and had to use the fields.

WATER SAFETY

The ancient Egyptians taught their children to swim, which was important living so close to the Nile River. They also believed in magic, so they made their children wear charms (or small objects) to save them from drowning. They believed it was important to do both of these things.

Most towns had several doctors, and a surgeon working with them. We know how these doctors worked because some of their medical books have survived. Doctors used herbal medicines on their patients. For example, they gave willow bark pills for pain. Willow has the same chemicals in it as the aspirin we use today. At the same time as they gave the herbal cures, doctors said a magic spell over the patient.

This detail of a carving shows an ancient Egyptian surgeon's tools. Surgeons dealt only with serious disorders or injuries. Surgery was dangerous and likely to kill the patient, so it was done only when there was no other option.

Religion

The ancient Egyptians believed in many different gods and goddesses, who affected their daily lives and also judged them in the **afterlife.**

The important gods and goddesses had several jobs. For example, the goddess Hathor was the goddess of love and also of music and childbirth. It was important to keep these gods and goddesses happy. This is why people built **temples** from stone— because the gods would need them to live in forever.

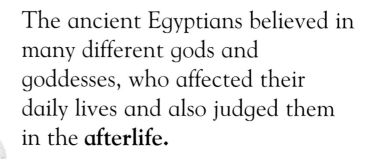

Gods and goddesses were important to the ancient Egyptians. So was preparing for the afterlife. People were buried with *shabti* figures like this one, to do their work in the afterlife.

This boat was buried next to the pyramid of the pharaoh Khufu, as part of the treasure for him to take to the afterlife.

Everyone believed that as long as they had led a good life in this world, they would be rewarded after death. They were buried with things for the afterlife. The **pharaoh** had the most expensive belongings. The **pyramids** of Egypt are tombs for some of the pharaohs. Each tomb is mostly underground, with many false passages and blocked walls, to stop people from robbing the treasure inside. Most people were simply buried in the hot desert sand.

Food

Ancient Egyptian townspeople all ate a lot of bread and drank a thick, weak beer made from stale barley. They had more choice of what to eat than people in small villages, because they could trade food. They ate onions, cucumbers, beans, and other vegetables each day. They kept sheep, goats, and cows for milk and cheese. Only the **pharaoh** and wealthy people ate meat each day.

When animals were killed, they had to be eaten quickly, before the heat made the meat go bad. This ancient Egyptian wall painting shows animals being butchered.

Egyptian recipe—nut candy

This recipe for candy probably comes from the very end of the ancient Egyptian period. It was written on a piece of broken pottery. As few women —who mostly did the cooking—could read or write, most recipes were just memorized, not written down.

WARNING: Ask an adult to help you with the cooking.

You will need:
1/2 cup of
   chopped dates
some hot water
a pinch of
   cinnamon
1/6 cup walnuts
   (or pecans),
   chopped
1 tablespoon of
   honey
2 tablespoons of
   ground almonds

1 Mash up the chopped dates with about a teaspoon of hot water.
Mix it until it is quite smooth.

2 Stir in the chopped nuts until they are well mixed with the dates.

3 Take a teaspoon of the mixture at a time and shape it into a ball. If it is too sticky, add some ground almonds.

4 Put the honey on a plate and roll the balls in it until they are coated in honey all over.

5 Now roll the sticky balls in the ground almonds.

Egyptian Towns Now

Egyptian towns are still mainly built along the Nile River. Many of them are built on top of, and around, ancient towns. The mud brick buildings have crumbled and have been replaced many times over thousands of years. Today, towns are full of concrete and stone buildings. A **dam** has been built on the Nile, to stop the yearly flooding. So towns are able to be built right next to the riverbanks.

The **pyramids** near the modern capital of Egypt, Cairo, were built almost 4,500 years ago. They housed tombs for the **pharaohs** who ruled from the nearby ancient town of Memphis.

Glossary

afterlife where the Egyptians believed people went after they died

apprentice young person who works with an experienced craftsperson to learn a skill such as shoemaking

archaeologist person who uncovers old buildings and burial sites to find out about the past

awning cloth cover to keep off sunlight or rain

bronze tough, strong metal made by melting together two softer metals, copper and tin

courtyard open space within, or on one side of, a building

dam wall built across a river to hold back the flowing water. Dams often have gates or pipes to let through some of the held back water a little at a time.

duty work set number of days each year that people had to work for the pharaoh. Scribes did not have to do this work, but everyone else did.

fertile rich, good for growing things

linen cloth made from flax

official person who helps run a country

pharaoh ruler of ancient Egypt

priest/priestess man/woman who works in a temple, serving a god or goddess

pyramid tomb for a pharaoh, built between about 2650 B.C.E. and 1750 B.C.E. Before and after this, pharaohs were buried in different kinds of tombs.

scribe person in ancient Egypt who could read or write. Scribes helped officials and pharoahs run the country.

shrine place where people come to pray to gods and goddesses and leave them gifts

temple large building where many people pray together to gods and goddesses and leave them offerings

trade job, such as shoemaking

tunic long T-shirt-shaped clothing

More Books to Read

Alcraft, Rob. *Visiting the Past: Valley of the Kings.* Chicago: Heinemann Library, 1999.

Shuter, Jane. *Ancient Egypt: Builders and Craftsmen.* Chicago: Heinemann Library, 1999.

Thames, Richard. *Ancient Egyptian Children.* Chicago: Heinemann Library, 2002.

Williams, Brenda. *Ancient Egyptian Homes.* Chicago: Heinemann Library, 2002.

Williams, Brian. *The Life and World of Tutankhamun.* Chicago: Heinemann Library, 2002.

Index